"The Siwak is a cleanser of the mouth and a pleasure to the lord." al-Bukhari, an-Nasai, Ahmad

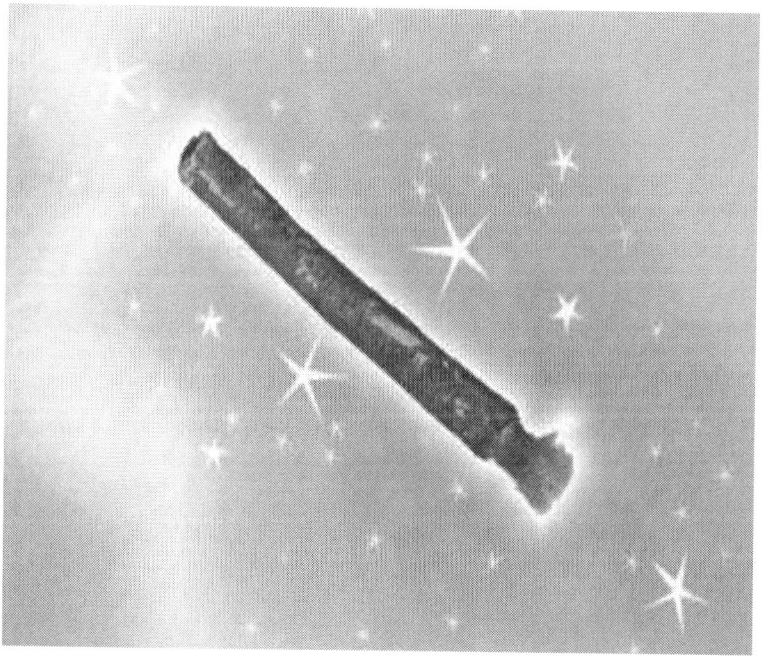

SIWAK - MISWAK

THE MIRACLE BRUSH

Fisabilillah Organization Authenticate Ulama's Organization
Published By: The Way of Islam, 6 Cave Street, Preston, Lancashire, PR1 4SP

CONTENT

PREFACE

It is Allāh's infinite mercy upon us that He has made us part of the complete and perfect religion of Islām. The religion with the perfect Qur'ān, and the perfect Messenger ﷺ.

We, as Muslims, believe in the example of the Messenger, Muḥammad ﷺ, to be the best example to follow if we wish to become successful in the truest meaning of the word. This example is not limited to only acts of worship, but rather, it covers the entire manner in which we live our lives. In fact, Islām in being a complete way of life has received all manners of praise from the time of the Messenger ﷺ, till the present day.

What should also be noted by Muslims and non-Muslims alike, is that it was the teachings of Islām regarding cleanliness that had started the sciences of medicine and hygiene. Unfortunately, however, it is sad to see that Muslims are extremely quick to forget the greatness that Islām gives them as they readily abandon the teachings of Islām in favour of the outwardly pleasing alternatives provided by others.

One such item that is largely disregarded by Muslims is the Siwāk (also known as Miswāk) or the tooth-stick. This is considered by some to even be barbaric or, at best, primitive. Just scratching the surface reveals that what has been approved of and enforced by the Messenger ﷺ over 1400 years ago, still, in our present times, remains unsurpassed, in terms of availability, cost, and the actual benefit that it provides.

It is hoped that this publication will open the eyes of the readers to understand and appreciate the Sunnah of the Messenger ﷺ and to adopt it as an integral part of our lives. The benefit of this is as those who follow the example of the Messenger ﷺ at the time of widespread corruption, i.e. the reward of a martyr. Musnad al-Firdaws, aṭ-Ṭabarānī

INTRODUCTION

All praise is to Allāh, the Lord of the worlds, and peace and blessings be upon the final messenger Muḥammad, his family, his companions, and those who follow him by performing righteous deeds until the Day of Judgement.

In an age of modernity, many consider the way of life offered to us by the West to be superior and more worth-while in living. However, when the light emerged from the city of Makkah fourteen hundred years ago there was a turn of direction in the future of the world. Man was given divine guidance in order to lead his life in harmony with himself and nature. This guidance comprised of the Revelation from the heavens, and the example of the best man to walk upon the earth.

The blessed Messenger of Allāh ﷺ was the beloved of the Almighty, and as such every one of his actions was so beloved to Allāh that He promises His love to those who follow in the Prophet's footsteps: "Say, (O Muḥammad, to mankind): If you do indeed love Allāh, follow me; Allāh will love you and forgive for you your sins. Allāh is Forgiving, Merciful" (Qur'ān, 3:31).

Muḥammad, the Rasūlullāh, ﷺ was sent as a guide and teacher to mankind. He taught humanity how to live a dignified life, pleasing to the Creator and pleasing to creation, regardless of how humble one's surroundings. The Prophet's teachings were timeless; purity of body and mind, and of heart and soul were addressed with the same emphasis. The human being is, after all, both spirit and flesh; the religion of Fiṭrah – the uncorrupted natural state of man – created "a people of the middle way" (Qur'ān, 2:143) by its balance of earthly and heavenly, and its message that godliness can only be made up of both. And so matters of personal hygiene were not only taught by the Prophet ﷺ but actually incorporated as integral parts of worship.

SIWĀK – THE MIRACLE BRUSH

The Siwāk is one tool of hygiene which holds particular importance in Islām. It is a simple twig for cleaning the teeth, originating from the desert but popularised for ever more by the example and directives of the Messenger of Allāh ﷺ. It is no exaggeration to say that Rasūlullāh ﷺ is the first dental educator in proper oral hygiene in history. The Prophet's Siwāk of choice was from the Arāk (Aloes tree or Salvadora Persica).

The Siwāk is a natural twig fortified with natural minerals that help clean the teeth, other inhibitors that prevent gums from bleeding, cleaning agents that kill microbes and germs and remove plaque, and a scent that gives breath a naturally fresh smell. The Siwāk is an ideal, natural brush that has been endowed with more than any artificial toothpaste could ever have. The wicks on the Siwāk clean between the teeth and do not break under any amount of pressure; rather, they are flexible and strong. The small wicks bend to the appropriate shape to get plaque and leftover food out from in between teeth while avoiding any damage to the gums.

The Siwāk is comprised of many beneficial ingredients. Most significant among them are:

- Antibacterial acidic inhibitors that fight decay. They are natural disinfectants and can be used to stop bleeding. They disinfect the gums and teeth and close any microscopic cuts that may have existed in the gums. On first usage, the Siwāk will taste harsh, and maybe even burn, because of a mustard-like substance found in it, but this is the ingredient that fights decay in the mouth and kills germs.
- Minerals such as sodium chloride, potassium, sodium bicarbonate and calcium oxides. These clean the teeth. The American Dental

Association considers sodium bicarbonate to be a preferred ingredient in toothpastes.

- Natural scented oils that taste and smell nice, give the mouth a pleasant smell. They make up about 1% of the Siwāk.
- Enzymes that prevent the build-up of plaque that causes gum disease. Plaque is also the no. 1 cause of premature loss of teeth.
- Anti-decay and anti-germ ingredients that act as a penicillin of sorts, decreasing the amount of bacteria in the mouth, which means cleaner teeth and cleaner air when breathing through the mouth.

The presence of these properties has actually encouraged some toothpaste laboratories to incorporate powdered stems and/or root material of Salvadora Persica in their products.

The Importance of Siwāk in the Sunnah

Ā`ishah ﵂ narrates that Rasūlullāh ﷺ said, "Ten things are from the fiṭrah (man's natural disposition):

1) trimming the moustache,
2) lengthening the beard,
3) using the Siwāk,
4) cleaning out the nostrils with water,
5) clipping of the nails,
6) washing the joints of the fingers,
7) removing hair from under the armpits,
8) shaving the pubic hair,
9) washing the private parts,"
10) Muṣ`ab, a sub-narrator, said, "I have forgotten the tenth thing, unless it was the gargling of the mouth."

Muslim

Imām an-Nawawī states in his commentary of Saḥīḥ Muslim, "According to a majority of scholars (the word 'fiṭrah') refers to these ten things which are Sunnah, as stated by (Imām) al-Khaṭṭābī. It is also said that it refers to the practice of all the prophets, it is also claimed to mean religion, but this opinion is somewhat weak."

The Sunnah of the Ambiyā' (Prophets)

Malīḥ ibn `Abdullāh al-Khātamī narrates from his father who narrates from his grandfather that the Prophet ﷺ said, "Five things are from the Sunnah (practice) of the prophets: modesty, forbearance, cupping, using the Siwāk, and applying `iṭr (scent)." aṭ-Ṭabrānī in al-Kabīr

Abū Ayyūb ﵁ also mentions using the Siwāk and marriage from the Sunnah of the prophets. at-Tirmidhī

The fact that the Siwāk has been the practice of the noblest segment of humanity, namely the prophets of God, is sufficient to illustrate its value and to warrant it being adopted. On the other hand, those who miss out on this Sunnah deprive themselves of the blessings and barakah of this meritorious deed.

Acts of Cleanliness

Abū ad-Dardā' ﵁ reports that the Prophet of Allāh ﷺ said, "There are four acts of cleanliness:

1) to trim the moustache,
2) to remove the hair below the navel,
3) to cut the fingernails, and
4) to use the Siwāk." Majma` az-Zawā'id

In this Ḥadīth the Prophet highlights four acts of cleanliness, not to suggest that cleanliness is restricted to these four acts, but to demonstrate their prominence by giving them particular mention.

The Reward of Using a Siwāk

It has been reported by Ibn `Umar ﷺ that Rasūlullāh ﷺ said, "The Siwāk is a cleanser of the mouth and brings the pleasure of the Lord."

al-Bukhārī, an-Nasa'ī, Aḥmad

This Ḥadīth states two benefits, one for this world and one for the hereafter. The worldly benefit is that the offensive odour of the mouth is removed by the use of the Siwāk. The benefit of the Hereafter is that a person obtains the pleasure of Allāh, which is the objective of life.

Ā`ishah ﷺ narrates that Prophet ﷺ said, "The excellence of a Ṣalāh for which Siwāk is used compared to a Ṣalāh for which Siwāk is not used is seventy times over."

al-Ḥākim, Ibn Khuzaymah

Emphasis of Using the Siwāk

Abū Umāmah ﷺ has reported that Rasūlullāh ﷺ said, "Use the Siwāk, for the Siwāk is a cleansing for the mouth and it is beloved to the Lord. Jibrīl never came to me except that he counselled me regarding the Siwāk, until I feared that it may become compulsory upon my Ummah and me."

Ibn Mājah

Abū Hurayrah ﷺ reports that Rasūlullāh ﷺ has said, "Had it not been for placing my Ummah in difficulty, I would have commanded them to use the Siwāk at the time of each Ṣalāh."

al-Bukhārī

This Ḥadīth demonstrates that the Siwāk is not a Wājib (obligatory act). However, the great emphasis placed on the Siwāk, and on maintaining oral hygiene in general, can be clearly seen by the very direct wording used. Only for the concern of placing his Ummah in difficulty did the Prophet ﷺ decide not to issue an order for the Siwāk to be utilised prior to every Ṣalāh, otherwise it would have become a Wājib. Among the Ṣaḥābah, Zayd ibn Khālid ؓ is recorded as making a practice of coming to the Masjid with his Siwāk behind his ear and using it when getting up to pray.

at-Tirmidhī, Abū Dāwūd

Ibn `Abbās ؓ narrates from the Nabī ﷺ, "I was so persistently commanded about the Siwāk that I thought Qur'ānic Revelation or inspiration would be revealed regarding it."

al-Ḥākim

The Significance of Siwāk for the Prophet

It is transmitted in Sunan Abū Dāwūd that the Messenger ﷺ was initially commanded to renew his Wuḍū' for every Ṣalāh, whether or not he had it. However, when he experienced some difficulty he was given a concession regarding the Wuḍū' but commanded to maintain the use of the Siwāk for every Ṣalāh.

Times When the Use of the Siwāk is Particularly Recommended

The Aḥādīth below demonstrate how frequently the Messenger of Allāh ﷺ would use his Siwāk, thus making repeated use of the Siwāk a clearly established Sunnah. It is a fact that plaque begins to form immediately after meticulous brushing, so that by the end of a 24 hour period of time plaque is well on its way towards maturation and starts to harm the gums. Thanks to the repeated use of Siwāk during the day in following in the footsteps of the Messenger of Allāh ﷺ, Muslims traditionally showed (and, in many 'backward' regions of the world, still show) an unusually high level of oral cleanliness. This is not always the case with those whose oral hygiene only consists of brushing with a toothbrush as it is very unpractical to use a toothbrush and paste multiple times throughout the day or night.

Siwāk Before Sleeping

Ibn `Abbās ♦ narrates, "When Rasūlullāh ﷺ would wake up at night he would use the Siwāk." at-Ṭabarānī

In another Ḥadīth, Abū Hurayrah ♦ reports that the Prophet ﷺ did not go to sleep nor did he wake up except that he would use the Siwāk. at-Ṭabarānī

While the chain of narrators of this Ḥadīth may be weak according to Imām al-Haythamī because of one of the narrators, Muḥammad ibn `Amr, its contents are easily established by the many other Aḥādīth on the subject, some of which follow. Also, Imām Aḥmad has reported that this was the practice of Abū Hurayrah ♦, the primary narrator.

Using the Siwāk Upon Awakening During the Night

Ḥudhayfah ♦ narrates that when the Prophet ﷺ would wake up in the night he would clean his mouth with a Siwāk. al-Bukhārī

`Ā'ishah ♦ says, "I used to keep three red vessels for Rasūlullāh ﷺ at night, one contained water for Wuḍū', the second for his Siwāk and the third contained drinking water." Ibn Mājah

Ibn `Umar ♦ says that Rasūlullāh ﷺ never spent a night without using a Siwāk. at-Ṭabarānī

These Aḥādīth once again reveal the part the Siwāk played in the life of the final Prophet ﷺ and the importance he attached to it even in the darkness of the night he would make sure that he had a Siwāk nearby.

Siwāk Upon Awakening

It has been narrated by `Ā'ishah ﵂ that whenever Rasūlullāh ﷺ would wake up during the day or the night from sleep he would use the Siwāk before performing Wuḍū'.

Abū Dāwūd

Based on this Ḥadīth, Imām an-Nawawī states that it is Mustaḥabb to use Siwāk at all times; however, there are five times when this becomes desired even more, one of these is after waking up.

Buraydah narrates that whenever Rasūlullāh ﷺ woke up at home he would ask his maidservant, Barīrah, to bring a Siwāk.

Muṣannaf Ibn Abī Shaybah

Using the Siwāk at the Time of Tahajjud

Hudhayfah ﵁ narrates that whenever Rasūlullāh ﷺ would wake up at night, he brushed his teeth with a Siwāk.

al-Bukhārī

`Abdullāh ibn `Abbās ﵄ once spent the night with the Messenger of Allāh ﷺ. He saw him get up three times during the night, and at each time the Prophet ﷺ brushed his teeth with his Siwāk, made Wuḍū', recited from the 190th verse of Sūrah Āl `Imrān to the end of the Sūrah, and then offered two lengthy rak`ahs of Ṣalāh before lying back down and sleeping for a while. At the last time he offered his Witr Ṣalāh after two rak`āt of Tahajjud.

Abū Dāwūd

Using the Siwāk after Tahajjud

It is reported from Ibn `Abbās ﷺ that Rasūlullāh ﷺ would perform two rak`āts at a time at night. After every two rak`āts he would use the Siwāk.
Muṣannaf Ibn Abī Shaybah

`Ā'ishah ﷺ reports that they would put a Siwāk near the Prophet's water for Wuḍū'. She once said to the Prophet ﷺ, "You never seem to stop using the Siwāk." He said, "Yes, if it was possible for me to use it after every two rak`ahs of prayer I would surely do so."
Abū Ya`lah

To Perform Siwāk Before Dawn

It is reported by `Abdullāh ibn `Amr ﷺ that the Messenger ﷺ said, "If I did not think that it would burden my Ummah, I would certainly have commanded them to use the Siwāk at the time of dawn."
ad-Durr al-Manthūr with a reference to Abū Nu`aym

This Ḥadīth again reveals the emphasis of the Siwāk within Islām and the mercy of the Prophet for his Ummah. One should see the Siwāk as a vital tool in his or her life as this Ḥadīth indicates.

To Perform Siwāk When Entering The House

`Ā'ishah ﷺ said, "The very first action of the Messenger ﷺ when entering the home was Siwāk."
Aḥmad

Imām al-Manāwī states the reason for making Siwāk then as follows in his book, al-Fayḍ al-Qadīr:

"When the Prophet would enter his house," i.e. when intending to enter he would begin with Siwāk because of performing Salām to his family, as the name 'as-Salām' is a noble Name (of Allāh's). Another reason for using the Siwāk is the inevitable meeting and conversation with family members and in the case of the wife, if the husband wished to kiss her, there will be no ill odour emanating from his mouth, which can be upsetting."

To Use the Siwāk Before and After Eating

Abū Hurayrah ﷺ relates, "I began using the Siwāk before going to sleep and after awakening, and before and after meals ever since I heard the Prophet ﷺ say what he had said regarding it."
al-Bayhaqī

The Use of the Siwāk before the Recitation of the Qurān

`Alī ﷺ said, "Indeed your mouths are the pathways for (the recitation of) the Qur'ān, therefore cleanse and purify them with the aid of the Siwāk."
Ibn Mājah

To Use the Siwāk on Friday

Abū Sa`īd ﷺ reports that the Prophet ﷺ said, "On the day of Jumu`ah (Friday) it is necessary for every mature person that he bathes, cleans his teeth, and also that he apply some fragrance if he can find some."
Ibn Khuzaymah

It has been narrated from Abū Hurayrah ﷺ that Rasūlullāh ﷺ said, "Whoever bathes on Friday, uses the Siwāk, applies perfume if he has it, wears his best clothes, comes to the Masjid and does not stride over the shoulders of (seated) people, performs whatever Ṣalāh Allāh wills for him to perform, and when the Imām emerges he becomes silent, this will be an expiation (of sins) for him between this Friday and the previous one." Abū Hurayrah ؓ further states, "and three days extra, as Allāh multiplies all good deeds by ten."

al-Ḥākim

The aforementioned Ḥadīth outlines some of the etiquettes for Fridays, all of which are highly important. Moreover, we can see that when an important day such as Friday comes, the Prophet ﷺ specifically addresses the need to use the Siwāk, which entails a greater reward exclusive to that day.

In another narration by Abū Ayyūb ؓ, it is recorded that Rasūlullāh ﷺ said, "Whosoever comes for (the Jumu`ah) Ṣalāh on Friday should take a bath. If he has perfume (`iṭr), he should use it. And make this Siwāk compulsory upon yourself."

aṭ-Ṭabrānī

As a result of such emphasis, some scholars are of the opinion that Siwāk on the day of Jumu`ah is necessary (farḍ), such as Ibn Ḥazm. The general consensus of scholars, however, remains that it is a Mustaḥabb on Fridays too.

`Umdah al-Qārī

Siwāk in the State of Iḥrām

It is reported from Ibn `Abbās ؓ that the Rasūl ﷺ underwent cupping while being in the state of Iḥrām. Asked whether he used a Siwāk in the state of Iḥrām, Ibn `Abbās ؓ replied, "Yes."

Ibn Khuzaymah

The Siwāk of Women

It is reported from Yazīd ibn al-Aṣamm that Maymūnah's ؓ Siwāk was always placed in a container. If she was not engaged in Ṣalāh or some other work, she would use the Siwāk.

Muṣannaf Ibn Abī Shaybah

This Ḥadīth shows that Siwāk is a Sunnah for women just as it is for men and, therefore, women should follow the example of the Mother of the Believers, Maymūnah ﵂.

To Use Another Person's Siwāk

The Ḥadīth narrated by `Ā'ishah ﵂ about the Prophet's ﷺ last moments (see below) mentions that `A'ishah ﵂ gave the Messenger ﷺ her brother, `Abdur Raḥmān's ﵁ Siwāk to use. This Ḥadīth clearly illustrates the fact that one is allowed to use another person's Siwāk with the consent of the owner, which in this case was given by tacit approval from `Abdur Raḥmān ﵁.

Siwāk – A Provision for Travelling

`Ā'ishah ﵂ narrates that when the Prophet ﷺ would travel he would carry a Siwāk, comb, kohl bottle, bottle, and mirror. ad-Durr al-Manthūr

Once again it is quite evident that the Prophet considered the Siwāk an indispensable tool, whether at home or away.

Keeping a Siwāk Nearby

Abū Salamah ibn `Abdir Raḥmān reports that Zayd ibn Khālid ﵁ would keep his Siwāk behind his ear, "where a writer keeps his pen" so that he could use it before prayers. at-Tirmidhī, Abū Dāwūd

Siwāk at the Time of Death

`Ā'ishah ﵂ narrates, "When the Messenger ﷺ passed away in my house, during my turn (to be with him), it was from amongst the favours of Allāh upon me that while his head was between my bosom and lap, and before his passing away, Allāh combined my saliva and his saliva. (This was because) `Abdur Raḥmān ibn Abī Bakr ◈ came into my chamber with a Siwāk in his hand, while I was supporting the Apostle of Allāh ﷺ. I noticed him looking towards it and knew how much he loved the Siwāk, so I asked, 'Should I get the Siwāk for you?' He nodded his head and indicated 'yes'. I handed it to him but he found it too hard, so I asked, 'Shall I soften it for you?' He nodded his head once again, indicating 'yes'. I chewed it with my teeth till it became soft. The Messenger of Allāh ﷺ then began using it. Beside him was a pot of water. He immersed both his hands into the water, and rubbed it over his face saying, 'There is no god but Allāh, verily death has many difficulties!' Then he lifted his hand and repeatedly said, 'In the Highest Company!' (i.e. he asked to be taken to the company of the Messengers and Prophets before him) until his soul was taken away and his hand fell to his side."

al-Bukhārī

This Ḥadīth shows very clearly the importance of Siwāk, that at such a critical time, when in the jaws of death and while undergoing its difficulties, the Messenger of Allāh ﷺ should want so much to use the Siwāk. This noble Sunnah therefore had the honour of being one of the last actions carried out by him in his worldly life, ﷺ.

Benefits of Siwāk

Hisān ibn `Aṭiyyah ◈ has reported that Wuḍū' is half of Īmān and Siwāk is half of Wuḍū'.

Muṣannaf Ibn Abī Shaybah

Siwāk Cleanses the Teeth

Ja`far ibn Abī Ṭālib ﵁ narrates that a group of people came to the Prophet ﷺ, and he said to them, "Why is it that I see you with yellow teeth? Use the Siwāk." Kitāb al-Āthār of Abū Yūsuf

Siwāk Strengthens the Memory

`Alī ﵁ relates, "Five things prevent memory loss and also decrease phlegm: Siwāk, fasting, recitation of the Qur'ān, honey, and milk".

ad-Daylamī

The Excellence of the Siwāk

Abū ad-Dardā' ﵁ states, "Make the use of the Siwāk compulsory upon yourself, use it constantly and do not neglect it," and then he goes on to mention many benefits of the Siwāk, including:

"The greatest and highest of its virtues is that the Most Merciful's pleasure is earned, and whoever attains Most Merciful's pleasure will enter Jannah.

"Secondly it is a Sunnah.

"Thirdly, the reward of prayer is increased by seventy times.

"Fourthly, wealth and provision are increased.

"Fifthly, it sweetens the smell of the mouth.

"Sixthly, it strengthens the gums and makes them firm.

"Seventhly, it relieves one from headaches.

"Eighthly, it eradicates the pain felt in the molars.

"Ninthly, the angels shake the hands of the person who uses it, because of the illumination seen on his face.

"Tenthly, it keeps one's teeth clean..." al-Fayḍ al-Qadīr

Ibn `Abbās ﷺ reports, "Make the use of the Siwāk necessary, for indeed it is a means of cleansing the mouth, attaining the pleasure of the Lord, and a cause of happiness for the angels. It increases one's reward, and is from the Sunnah, makes ones eyesight sharper, eradicates scurvy, strengthens the gums, diminishes phlegm, and creates a pleasant smell in the mouth." al-Bayhaqī in Shu`ab al-Īmān

SOME FIQH RELATED TO SIWĀK

Siwāk in Preparation for Ṣalāh

There is a difference of opinion between the jurists regarding the time of Siwāk before commencing Ṣalāh, which is based on the different meanings derived from the Aḥādīth. Is the Siwāk a Sunnah for Wuḍū' or Ṣalāh?

Most Ḥanafī scholars consider the Siwāk a Sunnah for Wuḍū', while the Shafi`ī school of thought considers the Siwāk a Sunnah for Ṣalah. The result of this difference manifests when a person performs a number of Ṣalāhs with one Wuḍū'. According to the Ḥanafī position, performing Siwāk once is sufficient for the Sunnah, while according to the Shafi`ī position, one should use the Siwāk afresh before every Ṣalāh.

However, some Ḥanafī scholars such as al-Ḥalabī regard the use of the Siwāk before Ṣalāh as preferable (Mustaḥabb), thereby removing the point of contention in this issue. However, when using the Siwāk before Ṣalāh, anyone that is a Ḥanafī should ensure that blood does not flow from the gums, as it would nullify Wuḍū' if it did. At such times, the Siwāk should be used carefully and only the teeth should be brushed with it, so that no blood flows from the gums.

When to Use the Siwāk During Wuḍū'

Furthermore, there is a difference of opinion about when one should make Siwāk in relation to Wuḍū'. Some scholars are of the opinion that it should be used when gargling the mouth, while other scholars assert that Siwāk should be performed before beginning Wuḍū`. Either way is equally valid, except it would be more practical to do it at the start of Wuḍū' for those who experience frequent gum bleeding.

al-Baḥr al-Rā'iq

The Siwāk Branch

All types of Siwāk are permissible as long as they do not cause one harm or pain in the mouth such as canes and reed. However, there are certain branches which are recommended by the Prophet ﷺ, which are as follows:

Arāk (Salvadore Persica)

Imām an-Nawawī states in Sharḥ Muslim that it is Mustaḥabb (desirable) to use a stick from the Arāk (Salvadore Persica) for Siwāk.

It is reported by `Abdullāh ibn Mas`ūd ؓ that he would pick the Arāk for the Prophet's Siwāk.

Musnad Abī Ya`lā

Zaytūn (Olive Tree)

Mu`ādh ibn Jabal ؓ narrates that he heard the Messenger ﷺ say, "A wonderful Siwāk is the Zaytūn, which is from a blessed tree. It cleanses the mouth and removes the yellowness from the teeth. This is my Siwāk and the Siwāk of the Prophets before me." at-Ṭabrānī in al-Awsaṭ

The Intention for Siwāk

One should have the intention of following the Sunnah when using the Siwāk.

Anas ibn Mālik ؓ relates that the Prophet ﷺ said, "There is no action for him who has no intention, and no reward for him who has no expectation."
al-Bayhaqī in al-Kubrā

The Manner of Using the Siwāk

The Siwāk should be held in the right hand, as it is narrated by `Ā'ishah ؓ, "The Prophet ﷺ liked to begin as much as he could with the right in the things he did, including attaining ritual cleanliness, combing his hair, and wearing his shoes."
al-Bukhārī

There is a general consensus that one should begin Siwāk from the right side of the mouth.
al-Insāf

According to the jurist Ibn Nujaym, the manner of using the Siwāk is as follows: The upper teeth and the palate should be brushed beginning on the right hand side and then the left at least three times, and then the same should be repeated with the lower teeth and palate. The Siwāk should be washed before beginning on a different area.
al-Baḥr ar-Rā'iq

The Siwāk should be used moderately (in force applied), because excessively hard brushing can cause the coating of the teeth to wear away and cause the teeth to become very sensitive.
Ibn Jawziyyah in aṭ-Ṭibb an-Nabawī

A Substitute when One Does Not have a Siwāk or Teeth

Anas ﷺ narrates that an Anṣārī asked the Prophet ﷺ, "O Messenger of Allāh, you have exhorted us to use the Siwāk. Is there an alternative in the absence of the Siwāk?" The Prophet ﷺ replied, "Your two fingers are your Siwāk when making Wuḍū', rub them against your teeth."

al-Bayhaqī

To use the fingers in place of Siwak while having the ability to use one will deprive a person of the reward of using a Siwāk.

The Siwāk should also be used if one has no teeth, the Siwāk should be rubbed gently against the gums. Likewise, the finger should also be used in the absence of a Siwāk, which is reported in the following Ḥadīth:

`Ā'ishah ﷺ asked Rasūlullāh ﷺ, "Should a person who has no teeth also make Siwāk?" Rasūlullāh ﷺ answered, "Yes." She asked, "What would he do?" He replied, "He should place his fingers in his mouth (for the purpose)."

aṭ-Ṭabrānī

Siwāk and the Toothbrush

Imām an-Nawawī states that though it is Mustaḥabb to use the branch of the Arāk tree for the purposes of a Siwāk, anything that eradicates the odour is in the ruling of Siwāk such as a rough cloth, sedge and glasswort.

Sharḥ Muslim

Thus anything that removes the ill odour and yellowness of teeth enables one to attain the reward of oral hygiene, which is a Sunnah in itself. However, the specific reward for using a Siwāk cannot be attained by using a toothbrush. Therefore one should at least make a point of using the Siwāk at certain times, such as during Wuḍū', in order to follow the way of the Messenger of Allāh ﷺ.

Some Recommendations for the Siwāk

1) The head (brush end) of the Siwāk should not be too soft or too hard, but should be moderate.
2) The Siwāk stick should not be twisted.
3) The length of the Siwāk should be a span's length or equal to the distance from the wrist to the tip of the middle finger to begin with. It does not matter if it becomes shorter later due to use.
4) To use a Siwāk which is from a harmful branch is not permissible.
5) To use or keep the Siwāk in the toilet is makrūh and unhygienic.
6) The Siwāk should not be used from both the ends.
7) The twigs of an unknown tree should not be used as a Siwāk as these could sometimes be poisonous.
8) The Siwāk should be stored with the brush tip facing upwards.
9) The fibres of the Siwāk should not be swallowed.
10) If one's gums are prone to bleeding then one should use the Siwāk while performing Wuḍū', rather than after it.

TRANSLITERATION GUIDE

Please take note of the table below as our transliteration method may be different to those adopted by others.

The transliterated symbols are unvarying in pronunciation, e.g. the representation "s" will remain pronounced as "s" and not distort to "z" in any circumstance, e.g. Islām is *not* pronounced Izlām.

While every effort has been made to ensure the transliteration is as close to the Arabic as possible, no alphabet can ever fully represent another.

This is all the more true where recitation of Qur'ānic verses is concerned as this must adhere to the very precise science of Tajwīd. It is therefore imperative that the readers do not consider a transliteration a substitute for learning to read Arabic correctly from a competent teacher.

VOWELS

A / a	SHORT "A" AS IN "AGO"	**I / i**	SHORT "I" AS IN "SIT"
Ā / ā	LONG "A" AS IN "HAT"	**Ī / ī**	LONG VOWEL AS IN "SEE"
AY or AI	DIPHTHONG AS IN "PAGE"	**AW or AU**	DIPHTHONG AS IN "HOME"
'	ABRUPT START/PAUSE DOES NOT OCCUR IN ENGLISH	**U / u**	SHORT "U" AS IN "PUT"
		Ū / ū	LONG VOWEL AS IN "FOOD"

CONSONANTS

ب	**B**	"B" NO "H" ATTACHED
ت	**T**	"T" NO "H" ATTACHED
ث	**TH**	"TH" AS IN THIN
ح	**Ḥ**	"H" GUTTURAL SOUND
خ	**KH**	"KH" VERY GUTTURAL NO TONGUE USAGE
د	**D**	"D" NO "H" ATTACHED
ذ	**DH**	"TH" AS IN THEN
س	**S**	"S" ONLY - NOT "Z"
ش	**SH**	"SH" AS IN SHIN
ص	**Ṣ**	"S" WITH RAISED TONGUE

ض	**Ḍ**	"DH" USING SIDES OF THE TONGUE
ط	**Ṭ**	"T" WITH RAISED TONGUE
ظ	**Ẓ**	"TH" AS IN THEN, SOUND IS WITH RAISED TONGUE
ع	**`**	GUTTURAL SOUND - ACCOMPANIES VOWEL
غ	**GH**	"GH" VERY GUTTURAL NO TONGUE USAGE
ق	**Q**	"K" WITH BACK OF TONGUE RAISED
و	**W**	"W" READ - NOT SILENT
ي	**Y**	"Y" ONLY - NOT "I"

Note: Double consonants must be pronounced with emphasis on both letters without pause, e.g. **ALLĀHUMMA** should be read **AL-LĀHUM-MA.**

SYMBOLS

سبحانه وتعالى	SUBḤĀNAHŪ WA TA`ĀLĀ FOR ALLAH "GLORIFIED AND EXALTED IS HE"	صلى الله عليه وسلم	ṢALLALLĀHU `ALAYHI WA SALLAM FOR MUHAMMAD "PEACE BE UPON HIM"
رضي الله عنه	RAḌIYAL-LĀHU `ANHU FOR COMPANIONS "ALLAH BE PLEASED WITH HIM"	عليه السلام	`ALAYHIS-SALĀM FOR PROPHETS "PEACE BE UPON THEM"

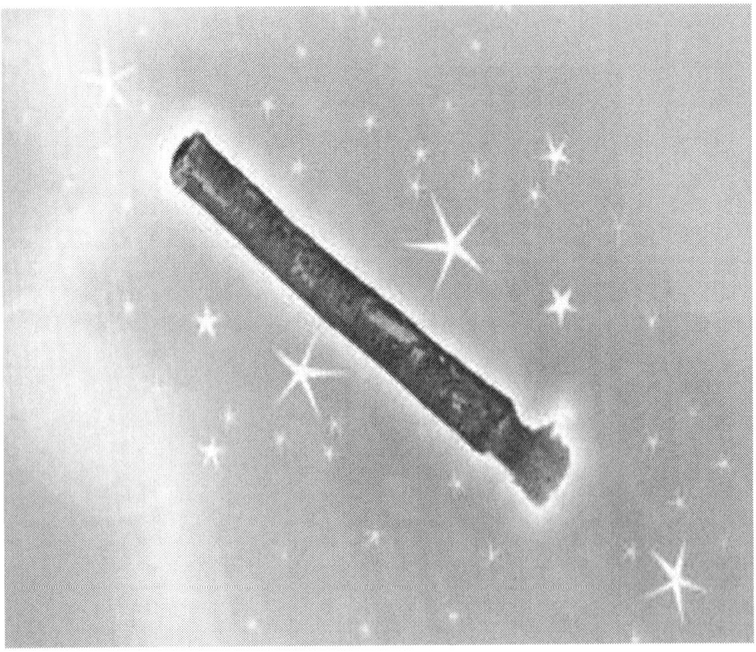

Made in the USA
Middletown, DE
21 March 2023

27307763R00015